COLLINS
Mental
Maths 4

Jan Henley

Collins Educational

An imprint of HarperCollinsPublishers

More and less

Answer the questions using these numbers.

| 2378 | 3009 | 6400 | 7099 | 8999 |

What is:

1. 1 more than each number?
2. 1 less than each number?
3. 10 more than each number?
4. 10 less than each number?
5. 100 more than each number?
6. 100 less than each number?
7. 1000 more than each number?
8. 1000 less than each number?
9. What is 10p more than £1.99?
10. What is 100 metres less than 5000 metres?
11. What is 1000 grams less than 2300 grams?
12. What is £1 less than 1002p?

Large and small

1. Which is more, 3214 or 3124?
2. Which is longer, 5019 metres or 5109 metres?
3. Which is colder, −5°C or −3°C?
4. Which is lighter, 8911 grams or 9191 grams?

Put these numbers in order, the smallest first.

5. 2678, 1876, 1786, 2876
6. 1091, 1009, 1900, 1901

Fill in the missing numbers so that all 5 numbers are in the correct order.

7. 4010, ☐, 4100, ☐, 4198
8. 5699, ☐, 5711, ☐, 5720
9. 8995, ☐, 9005, ☐, 9012

Write these temperatures in order, the lowest first.

10. 3°C, −6°C, 0°C, −4°C, 2°C

Write any number that would make these statements true.

11. 4230 < ☐ < 4300
12. 9099 > ☐ > 9090

Rounding to the nearest 10 and to the nearest 100

Round these numbers to the nearest 10.

1. 674
2. 458
3. 203
4. 975
5. 398
6. 707

> 723 is 720 rounded to the nearest 10 because it is nearer to 720 than to 730. Remember, we round *up* when a number is halfway between two tens.

Round these numbers to the nearest 100.

7. 624
8. 853
9. 909
10. 180
11. 971
12. 549

> 678 is 700 when rounded to the nearest hundred because it is nearer to 700 than to 600.

Number sequences

Write the next 2 numbers in each of these sequences and explain the rule.

1. 34, 40, 46, 52, ☐, ☐
2. 89, 86, 83, 80, ☐, ☐
3. 258, 251, 244, 237, ☐, ☐
4. 850, 840, 830, 820, ☐, ☐
5. 65, 56, 47, 38, ☐, ☐
6. 258, 250, 242, 234, ☐, ☐
7. 16, 12, 8, 4, ☐, ☐
8. −11, −8, −5, −2, ☐, ☐

Fill in the missing numbers in these sequences and explain the rule.

9. ☐, 231, 236, ☐, 246, ☐
10. −13, −7, ☐, ☐, 11, 17
11. 89p, 99p, ☐, £1·19, ☐, ☐
12. 1502, 1402, ☐, 1202, ☐,

Multiples

HELP BOX

Use the facts in the Help Box to answer these questions.
True or false?

- Multiples of 100 end in 00.
- Multiples of 10 end in 0.
- Multiples of 2 end in 0, 2, 4, 6 or 8.
- Multiples of 3: the sum of the digits can be divided exactly by 3.
- Multiples of 4: the last 2 digits can be divided exactly by 4.
- Multiples of 5 end in 0 or 5.

1. 42 is a multiple of 3
2. 1025 is a multiple of 5
3. 142 is a multiple of 4
4. 3090 is a multiple of 100
5. 2486 is a multiple of 2
6. Write all the multiples of 5 between 3448 and 3481.
7. Write all the multiples of 4 between 150 and 170.
8. Write all the multiples of 3 between 200 and 220.

7	13	16	27	34	48	62	75

9. Which of these numbers are multiples of 3?
10. Which of these numbers are multiples of both 2 and 4?

Factors and prime numbers

HELP BOX

Write all of the factors of these numbers:

1. 12
2. 9
3. 27
4. 32
5. 45
6. 24

18 has the factors:
1, 2, 3, 6, 9 and 18.
You can divide 18 by each of these numbers without leaving a remainder.

7. Which of these numbers has an odd number of factors? 16, 22, 31, 36, 40, 75, 100

Numbers with only two factors 1 and the number itself, are called *prime numbers* for example, 13 (factors 1 and 13).

Write the prime numbers in each set.

9. 4, 9, 17, 23, 27
10. 30, 35, 39, 41, 47

Write all the prime numbers between:

11. 20 and 30
12. 40 and 50

Square numbers

What is:

1. 4^2?
2. 1^2?
3. 10^2?
4. 6^2?

Which number multiplied by itself gives:

5. 9?
6. 64?
7. 49?
8. 81?

CHECK UP 1

1. What is 10 more than 799?
2. Round 547 to the nearest 10.
3. What is 7 squared?
4. 137 is a multiple of 3, true or false?
5. Which is lower, −4°C or −5°C?
6. What are the factors of 50?
7. Complete this sequence and explain the rule.
   22, 29, ☐, 43, ☐, 57
8. Write all the prime numbers between 10 and 20.
9. Write these in order, the largest first.
   £1·09, 99p, £0·90, £1·19
10. What is 1000 less than 1389?
11. What number gives 64 when multiplied by itself?
12. All multiples of 4 are even, true or false?
13. Round 398 to the nearest 10.
14. Write the next two numbers in this sequence.
    2092, 2094, 2096, 2098
15. Write any number that would make this statement correct.
    4390 < ☐ < 4450

Number bonds to 20

1. 13 add 6
2. $17 - 8 = \square$
3. 6 less than 13
4. Add 5 and 8
5. $12 + 8 = \square$
6. $15 - \square = 6$
7. 7 add 5
8. 6 more than 8
9. 11 subtract 4
10. What is the sum of 5 and 12?
11. $\square - 3 = 8$
12. 9 plus 4

Making 100

What do you have to add to each of these numbers to make 100?

1. 38
2. 57
3. 18
4. 65
5. 71
6. 43
7. 29
8. 32
9. 7
10. 64
11. 86
12. 41

Making 1000

What do you have to add to each of these numbers to make 1000?

1. 250
2. 470
3. 690
4. 520
5. 790
6. 130
7. 880
8. 620
9. 910
10. 340
11. 290
12. 710

Doubles and halves to 100

1. 23 + 23 = ☐
2. Double 36
3. 52 is double ☐
4. 17 + 17 = ☐
5. Half of 64
6. 39 + 39 = ☐
7. Double 48
8. 58 is double ☐
9. Half of 32
10. 27 + 27 = ☐
11. Half of 92
12. 49 + 49 = ☐

Doubles and halves of multiples of 10

1. 240 + 240 = ☐
2. 360 + 360 = ☐
3. Half of 540
4. 380 is double ☐
5. 460 = ☐ + ☐
6. 450 + 450 = ☐
7. Double 290
8. 680 is double ☐
9. 190 + 190 = ☐
10. Half of 940
11. Double 270
12. 490 + 490 = ☐

Doubles and halves of multiples of 100

1. 700 + 700 = ☐
2. Half of 2400
3. 5000 = ☐ + ☐
4. Double 3400
5. 5200 is double ☐
6. 1800 + 1800 = ☐
7. Half of 6800
8. Double 4600
9. 3900 + 3900 = ☐
10. 2700 + 2700
11. 8800 is double ☐
12. 5800 = ☐ + ☐

Near doubles

28 + 27 equals 55 because it is double 27 plus 1, or double 28 minus 1. You might also work it out as double 30 minus 5.

Now try these by identifying near doubles.

1. 36 + 38 = ☐
2. 25 + 27 = ☐
3. 150 + 160 = ☐
4. 47 + 48 = ☐
5. 29 + 27 = ☐
6. 470 + 460 = ☐

7. 340 + 350 = ☐
8. 47 + 46 = ☐
9. 480 + 460 = ☐
10. 17 + 15 = ☐
11. 290 + 270 = ☐
12. 49 + 48 = ☐

CHECK UP 2

1. 67 + ☐ = 100
2. ☐ + 12 = 20
3. Double 17
4. 35 + 36 = ☐
5. Half of 680
6. 550 + ☐ = 1000
7. 29 + 29 = ☐
8. 17 + 19 = ☐
9. 290 + ☐ = 1000
10. 37 + ☐ = 100
11. Half of 320
12. Double 4500

Counting on and counting back

Count on or back in ones to work these out.

1. 1004 – 7 = ☐

2. 1899 + 6 = ☐

3. 2995 + 8 = ☐

4. 5002 – 6 = ☐

Count on or back in tens.

5. 365 + 30 = ☐

6. 472 + 50 = ☐

7. 869 – 40 = ☐

8. 623 – 50 = ☐

This time, count on or back in hundreds.

9. 330 + 500 = ☐

10. 745 – 400 = ☐

11. 289 + 600 = ☐

12. 851 – 300 = ☐

Count up to the next multiple

HELP BOX

Work these out by counting up to the next multiple of 10
and then subtracting the amount you counted on.
For example: 47 + 25 = (47 + 3) + (25 – 3) because 47 + 3 is 50
= 50 + 22
= 72

Try these in the same way.

1. 28 + 17 = ☐

2. 56 + 25 = ☐

3. 37 + 66 = ☐

4. 49 + 36 = ☐

5. 68 + 24 = ☐

6. 76 + 18 = ☐

This time, count up to the next hundred.
For example: 398 + 13 = (398 + 2) + (13 – 2)
= 400 + 11
= 411

Now try these in the same way.

7. 495 + 16 = ☐

8. 297 + 15 = ☐

9. 596 + 8 = ☐

10. 789 + 13 = ☐

11. 692 + 12 = ☐

12. 391 + 21 = ☐

Tens then ones

Choose the strategy you prefer to work out these.

1. 43 + 38 = ☐
2. 37 + 45 = ☐
3. 28 + 54 = ☐
4. 17 + 75 = ☐
5. 45 + 28 = ☐
6. 76 + 18 = ☐
7. 23 + 56 = ☐
8. 62 + 19 = ☐
9. 57 + 28 = ☐
10. 38 + 25 = ☐
11. 44 + 28 = ☐
12. 55 + 37 = ☐

Check with a partner. Did they use the same strategy as you?
Can you explain your strategy?

Adding several numbers

1. 7 + 8 + 5 + 3 = ☐
2. 20 + 90 + 70 + 30 = ☐
3. 27 + 25 + 75 + 12 = ☐
4. 9 + 6 + 5 + 4 + 8 = ☐
5. 11 + 24 + 89 + 32 = ☐
6. 40 + 80 + 20 + 90 = ☐
7. 6 + ☐ + 8 + 4 = 23
8. 35 + ☐ + 65 = 149
9. ☐ + 30 + 90 + 50 = 220
10. 11 + ☐ + 5 + 9 = 31
11. 23 + ☐ + 77 + 11 = 125
12. 8 + 2 + 5 + 4 + 6 = ☐

Adding and subtracting 11, 21, 31...

1. 54 – 31 = ☐
2. 46 + 51 = ☐
3. 92 – 61 = ☐
4. Subtract 41 from 75
5. 89 – 41 = ☐
6. 58 plus 31
7. 41 more than 55
8. 60 – 31 = ☐
9. Take 71 away from 93
10. 37 add 51
11. 49 – 11 = ☐
12. 61 less than 89

HELP BOX

When adding 21 to a number add 20, then add on another 1. When subtracting 21 subtract 20, then take away another 1.

Adding and subtracting 9, 19, 29...

1. 45 – 19 = ☐
2. 57 + 39 = ☐
3. 62 take away 49
4. 29 more than 63
5. 58 plus 19
6. 72 – 49 = ☐
7. 31 subtract 19
8. 48 add 39
9. 59 less than 90
10. 77 + 19 = ☐
11. 33 + 59 = ☐
12. 64 – 39 = ☐

HELP BOX

When adding 19 to a number add 20, then subtract 1. When subtracting 19, take away 20 first, then add on 1.

Related facts

HELP BOX

Remember, if you know that 35 + 19 = 54, you also know that:

19 + 35 = 54

54 − 19 = 35 and 54 − 35 = 19

Work out the answer to these and then write 3 other related facts for each question.

1. 27 + 35 = ☐
2. 71 − 58 = ☐
3. 43 + 37 = ☐
4. 26 − 18 = ☐
5. 72 − 39 = ☐
6. 46 + 47 = ☐

Write 4 different sentences about each set of numbers.

7. 39, 12, 51
8. 93, 41, 52
9. 18, 44, 26
10. 29, 51, 22
11. 49, 45, 94
12. Use the numbers 35, 88, 42, 76 to write as many different addition and subtraction sentences as you can. How many can you write in 10 minutes?

CHECK UP 3

Explain the strategies you use to answer these questions.

1. 34 + 58 = ☐
2. 72 − 29 = ☐
3. 38 + 25 = ☐
4. 2003 − 7 = ☐
5. 87 − 21 = ☐
6. 68 + 29 = ☐

7. 35 + 26 + 11 + 65 = ☐
8. 432 − 50 = ☐
9. 5996 + 7 = ☐
10. 67 + 27 = ☐
11. 7 + 15 + 3 + 9 = ☐
12. 83 − 39 = ☐

Adding and subtracting multiples of 10

1. 30 + 80 = ☐
2. 57 + 40 = ☐
3. 254 – ☐ = 214
4. 70 + 40 = ☐
5. 129 + 60 = ☐
6. 130 – 60 = ☐
7. 150 – ☐ = 80
8. 36 + ☐ = 76
9. ☐ – 40 = 80
10. 342 + 50 = ☐
11. 194 – ☐ = 124
12. 140 – ☐ = 60

Adding and subtracting multiples of 100

1. 800 + 400 = ☐
2. 1500 – 800 = ☐
3. 700 + ☐ = 1300
4. ☐ – 600 = 500
5. 900 + 300 = ☐
6. ☐ + 600 = 1400
7. 1200 – ☐ = 700
8. 600 + ☐ = 1100
9. 1800 – 900 = ☐
10. 1700 – ☐ = 800
11. 800 + 500 = ☐
12. ☐ – 700 = 400

Adding to multiples of 10, 100 or 1000

1. 450 + 27 = ☐
2. 300 + 464 = ☐
3. 2000 + 458 = ☐
4. 720 + ☐ = 768
5. ☐ + 319 = 6319
6. 800 + 51 = ☐
7. 5000 + 102 = ☐
8. 70 + 28 = ☐
9. 2000 + ☐ = 2991
10. 560 + ☐ = 583
11. ☐ + 29 = 789
12. 610 + 81 = ☐

To the next 100

1. 269 + ☐ = 300
2. 745 + ☐ = 800
3. 426 + ☐ = 500
4. 121 + ☐ = 200
5. 313 + ☐ = 400
6. 877 + ☐ = 900
7. 609 + ☐ = 700
8. 555 + ☐ = 600
9. 938 + ☐ = 1000
10. 368 + ☐ = 400
11. 711 + ☐ = 800
12. 449 + ☐ = 500

To the next 1000

1. 5600 + ☐ = 6000
2. 3200 + ☐ = 4000
3. 1800 + ☐ = 2000
4. 4300 + ☐ = 5000
5. 8500 + ☐ = 9000
6. 2100 + ☐ = 3000
7. 6600 + ☐ = 7000
8. 8900 + ☐ = 9000
9. 7400 + ☐ = 8000
10. 700 + ☐ = 1000
11. 1100 + ☐ = 2000
12. 3400 + ☐ = 4000

CHECK UP 4

1. 345 + ☐ = 400
2. 70 + 50 = ☐
3. 4000 + ☐ = 4560
4. 7300 + ☐ = 8000
5. ☐ + 30 = 187
6. ☐ + 500 = 1300
7. ☐ + 54 = 273
8. 1400 − 600 = ☐
9. 96 − ☐ = 36
10. 8000 + ☐ = 8078
11. 6100 + ☐ = 7000
12. 1100 − ☐ = 300

Adding a single digit

1. 368 + 7 = ☐
2. 4154 + 8 = ☐
3. 785 + ☐ = 791
4. 5689 + ☐ = 5695
5. ☐ + 7 = 623
6. ☐ + 4 = 8211
7. 928 + 5 = ☐
8. 7029 + 8 = ☐
9. ☐ + 3 = 451
10. ☐ + 6 = 1923
11. 8738 + ☐ = 8742
12. 666 + ☐ = 672

Subtracting a single digit
from multiples of 100 or 1000

1. 500 − 6 = ☐
2. 8000 − 7 = ☐
3. 600 − ☐ = 592
4. 9000 − ☐ = 7998
5. ☐ − 3 = 197
6. 6000 − 9 = ☐
7. ☐ − 5 = 3995
8. 700 − ☐ = 692
9. 2000 − 4 = ☐
10. 300 − 9 = ☐
11. ☐ − 4 = 8996
12. ☐ − 7 = 993

Subtracting a single digit from any three- or four-digit number

Work these out and explain the strategies you used.

1. $672 - 3 = \square$
2. $346 - \square = 339$
3. $4321 - 4 = \square$
4. $8715 - \square = 8708$
5. $\square - 6 = 187$
6. $\square - 5 = 7769$
7. $181 - 7 = \square$
8. $306 - 9 = \square$
9. $6024 - \square = 6015$
10. $\square - 4 = 9008$
11. $\square - 8 = 989$
12. $3333 - 7 = \square$

Did you always use the same method?

What's the difference?

1. $6006 - 5998 = \square$
2. $3005 - 2991 = \square$
3. $8010 - 7998 = \square$
4. $5001 - 4983 = \square$
5. $3009 - \square = 12$
6. $9004 - \square = 7$
7. $\square - 1996 = 11$
8. $\square - 3985 = 16$
9. $2008 - 1989 = \square$
10. $\square - 6991 = 19$
11. $5012 - \square = 14$
12. $9004 - 8988 = \square$

HELP BOX

Find the difference between these pairs of numbers by counting on from the smaller number. For example:
$4002 - 3997 = 5$ because $3997 + 3 = 4000$ then another 2 makes 4002.

CHECK UP 5

1. 5001 − 4993 = ☐
2. 6000 − 2 = ☐
3. 4368 + ☐ = 4375
4. 400 − ☐ = 391
5. 2007 − ☐ = 1998
6. ☐ − 6 = 5994
7. 893 + 8 = ☐
8. ☐ + 5 = 3281
9. ☐ − 6997 = 12
10. 4000 − 7 = ☐
11. 7011 − 6999 = ☐
12. 5996 + 9 = ☐

Tables facts 1

1. Four fives
2. 7 x 3 = ☐
3. 9 x ☐ = 36
4. Multiply 6 by 10
5. How many 3s in 18?
6. 16 ÷ 4 = ☐
7. Divide 35 by 5
8. ☐ x 10 = 90
9. 8 x 4 = ☐
10. Multiply 9 by 5
11. Seven threes
12. 27 ÷ 3 = ☐

Mixed doubles and halves

1. 25 x 2 = ☐
2. 76 ÷ 2 = ☐
3. Double 160
4. Half of 700
5. 1600 x 2 = ☐
6. Twice 2300
7. 540 ÷ 2 = ☐
8. Double 39
9. 4700 x 2 = ☐
10. 3000 ÷ 2 = ☐
11. Half of 7200
12. 380 x 2 = ☐

Doubling and halving odd numbers

1. $\frac{1}{2}$ of 17
2. 23 ÷ 2 = ☐
3. Double $16\frac{1}{2}$
4. $9\frac{1}{2}$ x 2 = ☐
5. Half of 31
6. 39 ÷ 2 = ☐
7. Double $21\frac{1}{2}$
8. $15\frac{1}{2}$ x 2 = ☐
9. 41 ÷ 2 = ☐
10. ☐ ÷ 2 = $16\frac{1}{2}$
11. Double $19\frac{1}{2}$
12. 35 ÷ 2 = ☐

HELP BOX

Halving odd numbers will never give a whole number as an answer.

For example: 25 ÷ 2 = $12\frac{1}{2}$

Doubling and halving odd multiples of 10 and 100

HELP BOX

1. $\frac{1}{2}$ of 110
2. $90 \div 2 =$ ☐
3. Half of 170
4. ☐ x 2 = 150
5. Double 135
6. $190 \div 2 =$ ☐

When halving odd multiples of 10, for example 130, your answer will always have 5 in the units column. Half of 130 is 65.

You can always check you are right by doubling your answer.

Halving odd multiples of 100 will always give you an answer that ends in 50. For example, half of 1100 is 550. You might find it easier to halve the thousands first and then halve the hundreds.

7. Half of 1300
8. $900 \div 2 =$ ☐
9. ☐ x 2 = 750
10. $1900 \div 2 =$ ☐
11. Double 550
12. Half of 1700

Multiplying by 4

HELP BOX

1. 15 x 4 = ☐
2. 23 x 4 = ☐
3. 19 x 4 = ☐
4. 27 x 4 = ☐
5. 17 x 4 = ☐
6. 24 x 4 = ☐

To multiply by 4, try doubling the number and then doubling again. For example: 14 x 4 = 56 because double 14 is 28 and double 28 is 56.

Multiplying by 8

1. 9 x 8 = ☐
2. 6 x 8 = ☐
3. 8 x 8 = ☐
4. 4 x 8 = ☐
5. 7 x 8 = ☐
6. 3 x 8 = ☐

You can work out the 8 times table facts by doubling the facts you know from the 4 times table.

Multiplying by 10 or 100

1. 57 x 10 = ☐
2. 126 x 10 = ☐
3. 91 x 10 = ☐
4. 70 x 10 = ☐
5. ☐ x 10 = 850
6. ☐ x 10 = 3460

HELP BOX

When you multiply a number by 10, the digits move 1 place to the left.

For example: 43 x 10 = 430.

When you multiply a number by 100, the digits move 2 places to the left.

For example: 67 x 100 = 6700.

7. 39 x 100 = ☐
8. 71 x 100 = ☐
9. ☐ x 100 = 8500
10. 92 x 100 = ☐
11. ☐ x 100 = 5600
12. 40 x 100 = ☐

Dividing by 10 or 100

1. 3000 ÷ 10 = ☐
2. 6000 ÷ 100
3. ☐ ÷ 10 = 900
4. 7000 ÷ ☐ = 70
5. 2000 ÷ 100 = ☐
6. 4000 ÷ ☐ = 40
7. ☐ ÷ 100 = 50
8. 9000 ÷ 100 = ☐
9. ☐ ÷ 10 = 100
10. 8000 ÷ 100 = ☐
11. ☐ ÷ 100 = 50
12. 7000 ÷ 10 = ☐

HELP BOX

When dividing by 10, the digits move 1 place to the right. They move 2 places to the right when dividing by 100.

Multiplying by 5

1. 24 x 5 = ☐
2. 18 x 5 = ☐
3. 13 x 5 = ☐
4. 28 x 5 = ☐
5. 17 x 5 = ☐
6. 42 x 5 = ☐
7. 36 x 5 = ☐
8. 15 x 5 = ☐
9. 32 x 5 = ☐
10. 48 x 5 = ☐
11. 38 x 5 = ☐
12. 19 x 5 = ☐

HELP BOX

Try these by multiplying by 10 and then halving the result.

For example: 16 x 5 = (16 x 10) ÷ 2

= 160 ÷ 2

= 80

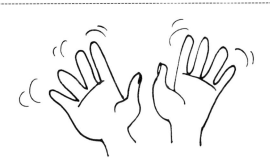

Multiplying by 20

1. 13 x 20 = ☐
2. 24 x 20 = ☐
3. 46 x 20 = ☐
4. 19 x 20 = ☐
5. 26 x 20 = ☐
6. 14 x 20 = ☐
7. 21 x 20 = ☐
8. 39 x 20 = ☐
9. 47 x 20 = ☐
10. 17 x 20 = ☐
11. 35 x 20 = ☐
12. 49 x 20 = ☐

HELP BOX

To multiply a number by 20, start by multiplying by 10 and then double your answer.

For example: 18 x 20 = (18 x 10) x 2

= 180 x 2

= 360

Double and double again

Copy and complete these multiplication sentences by doubling.

1. 1 x 15 = 15
   2 x 15 = ☐
   4 x 15 = ☐
   ☐ x 15 = 120
   16 x 15 = ☐

Continue this pattern to write 2 more multiplication sentences.

2. 1 x 12 = 12
   2 x 12 = ☐
   4 x 12 = ☐
   8 x 12 = ☐
   ☐ x 12 = 192

Can you continue the pattern to write the next 2 multiplication sentences? Write about the strategies you used to double the numbers.

Finding fractions by halving

Find a quarter of these numbers.

1. 84
2. 62
3. 96
4. 72
5. 600
6. 90

HELP BOX

You can find quarters of numbers by halving the number and then halving again. For example, a quarter of 60 is 15 because half of 60 is 30 and half of 30 is 15.

You can find an eighth of a number by halving it 3 times. For example: $\frac{1}{8}$ of 72 is 9 because half of 72 is 36, half of 36 is 18 and half of 18 is 9.

Find an eighth of these numbers.

7. 88
8. 200
9. 120
10. 56
11. 96
12. 180

CHECK UP 6

1. How many 3s in 18?
2. Half of 35
3. 17 x 5 = ☐
4. 56 x 10 = ☐
5. Quarter of 62
6. 1900 ÷ 2 = ☐
7. 7 x 8 = ☐
8. $\frac{1}{8}$ of 96

9. Double 850
10. Eight threes
11. 16 x 20 = ☐
12. 45 ÷ 5 = ☐
13. Double 29$\frac{1}{2}$
14. 78 x 100 = ☐
15. 990 ÷ 10 = ☐

Multiplying by 6

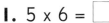

1. 5 x 6 = ☐
2. 9 x 6 = ☐
3. 7 x 6 = ☐
4. 3 x 6 = ☐
5. 6 x 6 = ☐
6. 4 x 6 = ☐

HELP BOX

You can work out the 6 times table facts by adding together the 2 times table facts and the 4 times table facts.
For example: 8 x 6 = (8 x 2) + (8 x 4)
= 16 + 32
= 48

Tables facts 2

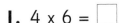

HELP BOX

These questions are about the 6, 7, 8 and 9 times tables. Remember, if you know that 8 x 3 = 24, you also know that 3 x 8 = 24.

1. 4 x 6 = ☐
2. How many 7s in 28?
3. 45 ÷ 9 = ☐
4. 3 x 9 = ☐
5. Multiply 4 by 8
6. What is 80 shared by 8?

7. 7 x 9 = ☐
8. 36 ÷ 6 = ☐
9. 18 divided by 9
10. Six sevens
11. 2 x 8 = ☐
12. How many 8s in 40?

Multiplying by 9

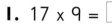

1. 17 x 9 = ☐
2. 13 x 9 = ☐
3. 16 x 9 = ☐
4. 11 x 9 = ☐
5. 14 x 9 = ☐
6. 20 x 9 = ☐
7. 24 x 9 = ☐
8. 18 x 9 = ☐
9. 12 x 9 = ☐
10. 25 x 9 = ☐
11. 38 x 9 = ☐
12. 30 x 9 = ☐

HELP BOX

To multiply a number by 9, multiply it by 10 first and then subtract the number.

For example: 15 x 9 = (15 x 10) − 15
$$= 150 − 15$$
$$= 135$$

Multiplying by 11

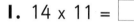

1. 14 x 11 = ☐
2. 16 x 11 = ☐
3. 15 x 11 = ☐
4. 17 x 11 = ☐
5. 18 x 11 = ☐
6. 21 x 11 = ☐
7. 36 x 11 = ☐
8. 24 x 11 = ☐
9. 23 x 11 = ☐
10. 29 x 11 = ☐
11. 42 x 11 = ☐
12. 43 x 11 = ☐

HELP BOX

To multiply a number by 11, multiply it by 10 first and then add the number to this.

For example: 17 x 11 = (17 x 10) + 17
$$= 170 + 17$$
$$= 187$$

Fractions

What is:

1. One tenth of 300?
2. $\frac{1}{4}$ of 32?
3. $\frac{1}{5}$ of 100?
4. Quarter of 400?
5. What fraction of £1 is 10p?
6. What fraction of 1 m is 25 cm?
7. What fraction of £5 is 50p?
8. What fraction of 1 cm is 1 mm?

9. What is $\frac{1}{4}$ of £2?
10. What is $\frac{1}{5}$ of 1 kg?
11. Which of these fractions are less than one half? $\frac{3}{8}$ $\frac{2}{4}$ $\frac{3}{4}$ $\frac{5}{8}$ $\frac{7}{8}$

Related facts

HELP BOX

> Remember, if you know that 15 x 9 = 135 you also know that:
> $$9 \times 15 = 135$$
> $$135 \div 9 = 15$$
> $$135 \div 15 = 9$$

Work out the answer to each of these questions then write 3 other related multiplication and division facts.

1. 21 x 3 = ☐
2. 19 x 9 = ☐
3. 32 ÷ 8 = ☐
4. 150 ÷ 10 = ☐
5. 27 x 11 = ☐
6. 200 ÷ 5 = ☐

Use these numbers to write 4 different multiplication and division sentences.

7. 3, 15, 45
8. 9, 27, 3
9. 170, 17, 10
10. 9, 8, 72
11. 100, 14, 1400
12. 20, 19, 380

Multiplying multiples of 10

1. 60 x 3 = ☐
2. 40 x 4 = ☐
3. 70 x ☐ = 350
4. 600 = 10 x ☐
5. 20 x ☐ = 100
6. 90 x 3 = ☐
7. ☐ x 4 = 240
8. 80 x ☐ = 400
9. 50 x 10 = ☐
10. 320 = ☐ x 4
11. 180 = ☐ x 3
12. 70 x 4 = ☐

Multiplying two-digit numbers

1. 16 x 4 = ☐
2. 32 x 5 = ☐
3. 19 x ☐ = 57
4. 34 x 3 = ☐
5. ☐ x 5 = 95
6. 44 x 3 = ☐
7. 26 x ☐ = 104
8. 18 x 4 = ☐
9. 92 = ☐ x 4
10. 17 x 5 = ☐
11. 39 x ☐ = 78
12. 54 x 4 = ☐

HELP BOX

Try strategies like multiplying the tens first and then the ones, or use the doubles facts you know to help with these. Write about the strategies you used.

CHECK UP 7

1. 8 multiplied by 6
2. ☐ x 3 = 96
3. 23 x 11 = ☐
4. 80 x ☐ = 400
5. Divide 42 by 6
6. 19 x 9 = ☐
7. How many 7s in 63?
8. 90 x ☐ = 360

9. 26 x 9 = ☐
10. 34 x 4 = ☐
11. ☐ x 6 = 240
12. Answer this question and then write 3 other multiplication or division related number sentences.
27 x 5 = ☐

Two operations

1. 40 = 18 x 2 + ☐
2. 23 x ☐ + 5 = 51
3. 40 x 6 + 9 = ☐
4. ☐ ÷ 5 + 7 = 16
5. 40 ÷ ☐ + 12 = 16
6. ☐ x 3 + 10 = 160
7. 98 = ☐ x 3 − 1
8. 27 + 13 ÷ 2 = ☐
9. 34 x ☐ + 5 = 141
10. 27 − 2 x 3 = ☐
11. ☐ x 5 + 8 = 408
12. ☐ ÷ 6 − 2 = 2

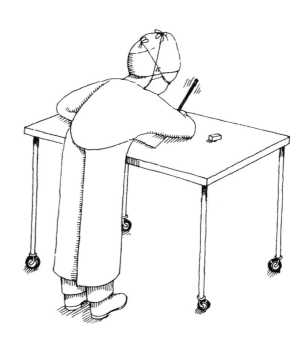

Puzzles

> The *sum* of two numbers is the answer you get when you add them together. The *product* is the answer you get when you multiply the two numbers together. For example: the sum of 8 and 4 is 12, the product of 8 and 4 is 32.

Find a pair of numbers with:

1. a sum of 15 and a product of 50
2. a sum of 8 and a product of 16
3. a sum of 30 and a product of 200
4. a sum of 12 and a product of 27

Choose digits from this set to complete these number sentences. You can use any digit more than once.

2	4	5	7

5. ☐☐ + ☐ = 61
6. ☐☐ − ☐ = 17
7. ☐☐ × ☐ = 110
8. ☐☐ ÷ ☐ = 5

Find the missing digits.

9. 2☐ + ☐0 = 77
10. ☐5 − 2☐ = 8
11. 3☐ × 4 = ☐☐4
12. ☐6 ÷ 2 = ☐8

Money

Work out mentally the total amount spent and how much change you would be given from £5 if you bought:

1. a pen and a rubber
2. a calculator, pencil and rubber
3. 2 pens and 2 pencils
4. a calculator and 3 pencils
5. all 4 items
6. How many pencils could you buy for £2?

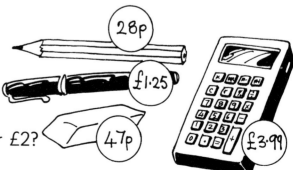

28p

£1·25

47p

£3·99

7. How many pens could you buy for £10?
8. Jake collected £24 for his sponsored swim. His dad gave him £6 of this. What fraction of the total amount did his dad give him?
9. A sticker album costs £1·50. If Shireen saves 30p a week, for how many weeks must she save to buy the album?
10. Luke spent a fifth of his savings on a book. If the book cost £2·50, how much had he saved?

Measures

How many:
1. centimetres in $5\frac{1}{2}$ metres?
2. grams in 2·5 kilograms?
3. millimetres in 27 centimetres?
4. millilitres in 10 litres?

Write:
5. 145 cm in metres
6. 6·5 m in centimetres
7. 9·5 cm in millimetres
8. 6·5 kg in grams

What is:
9. 5 kg + 250 g?
10. 60 cm and 4·5 m?

This recipe is to make 30 biscuits.

100 g margarine
75 g sugar
5 ml golden syrup
15 ml water
125 g flour

Write out the recipe for making:
11. 60 biscuits
12. 120 biscuits

Time

How many:

1. hours in 5 days?
2. years in 9 centuries?
3. minutes in four and a half hours?
4. years in 2 millenniums?
5. days in September, October and November?
6. weeks in 4 years?
7. Zoe leaves the house at 8:35 and arrives at school 17 minutes later. What time does she arrive?
8. A play at the theatre starts at 2:30 p.m. There are 2 acts, each lasting 45 minutes. There is a 20 minute interval. What time does the play end?

9. You have a 50 minute maths lesson each day at school. How long (in hours and minutes) do you spend doing maths each week?

10. How long does Rashid spend in bed?
11. Rashid's younger brother goes to bed 45 minutes earlier than Rashid. What time does he go to bed?
12. At the weekend Rashid goes to bed at 9 p.m. and gets up 45 minutes later than during the week. How long does he spend in bed?

CHECK UP 8

1. What two numbers have a sum of 10 and a product of 24?
2. A film starts at 7:35 p.m. and lasts for 75 minutes. What time does it end?
3. 32 x 3 + ☐ = 108
4. How many centimetres are there in 5·5 metres?
5. What is $\frac{1}{10}$ of £3?

6. Complete this sum: 7 x 4 + ☐ = 85
7. CDs cost £3·99. How many can you buy for £10? What change would you get?
8. How many days are there in 20 weeks?
9. 27 x ☐ + 9 = 63